MW00888352

BEST SON EVER

BLANK SKETCHBOOK

8.5 x 11 inches,
Sketch, Draw and Paint

110 Blank Pages

This book belongs to:

28990716R00063

Made in the USA
Lexington, KY
24 January 2019